A Crabtree Branches Book

Today's Stars

BILLIE EILISH

Samantha Bell

Crabtree Publishing

crabtreebooks.com

School-to-Home Support for Caregivers and Teachers

This high-interest book is designed to motivate striving students with engaging topics while building fluency, vocabulary, and an interest in reading. Here are a few questions and activities to help the reader build upon his or her comprehension skills.

Before Reading:

- *What do I think this book is about?*
- *What do I know about this topic?*
- *What do I want to learn about this topic?*
- *Why am I reading this book?*

During Reading:

- *I wonder why...*
- *I'm curious to know...*
- *How is this like something I already know?*
- *What have I learned so far?*

After Reading:

- *What was the author trying to teach me?*
- *What are some details?*
- *How did the photographs and captions help me understand more?*
- *Read the book again and look for the vocabulary words.*
- *What questions do I still have?*

Extension Activities:

- *What was your favorite part of the book? Write a paragraph on it.*
- *Draw a picture of your favorite thing you learned from the book.*

TABLE OF CONTENTS

A YOUNG SENSATION

Most people begin their careers after they finish school. Billie Eilish released her first hit when she was just 13 years old. She is a singer and songwriter. She is known for being able to connect with her listeners through her **lyrics**.

Billie Eilish attends the Met Gala at the Metropolitan Museum of Art in New York in 2022.

Billie is **passionate** about many things that young people face. She writes songs that reflect this. They have themes of loneliness, jealousy, and pain. Many people can relate to them.

Fun Facts

Billie has been a Justin Bieber fan since she was 12. She finally met him in 2019. He has helped her learn how to manage her fame.

Billie Eilish Pirate Baird O'Connell was born on December 18, 2001. She grew up in Los Angeles, California. Her parents are Maggie Baird and Patrick O'Connell. They homeschooled Billie and her older brother, Finneas, so they could pursue their interests.

Maggie Baird and Billie

Billie with her brother Finneas O'Connell at the 94th Academy Awards, March 27, 2022

Maggie taught Billie and Finneas the basics of songwriting. She wanted them to enjoy creating and writing music. By age six, Billie could play the **ukulele**. When she was eight, she joined a children's choir and improved her singing skills. By age 11, she was writing songs.

Billie playing the ukulele in 2017.

Fun Facts

Billie's first name honors her maternal grandfather, William. The name Eilish was inspired by a **documentary** her parents saw. Finneas chose the name Pirate.

GOING VIRAL

As Billie began writing songs, Finneas became her co-writer and **producer**. In 2015, she recorded a song for her dance teacher to use. The song was called "Ocean Eyes." Billie decided to upload it to SoundCloud, and it became her first **viral** hit.

Billie's next song was called "Six Feet Under." She uploaded it to SoundCloud in 2016, and it became a hit too. That year, she signed with Darkroom Records.

Fun Facts

Billie and Finneas wrote and recorded songs together in a room in their house.

Billie continued to release **singles** in 2017. She became the youngest artist to pass more than 1 billion streams on Spotify.

Billie at the premiere of the movie Everything, Everything *in 2017. Her song "Ocean Eyes" was part of the movie's* ***soundtrack****.*

STARDOM

In 2019, Billie released her first full-length album, ***When We All Fall Asleep, Where Do We Go?***

Soon after, she began winning awards. These included awards from the MTV Video Music Awards and the American Music Awards.

Billie at the 2021 MTV Video Music Awards at Barclays Center in Brooklyn, New York

Fun Facts

In 2021, Billie helped create a **vegan** Air Jordan shoe collection with Nike.

During the 2020 **Grammys**, Billie made music history. She became the first woman and the youngest artist to win the four biggest categories. She won Album of the Year, Record of the Year, Song of the Year, and Best New Artist.

Finneas and Billie arrive for the 62nd Annual Grammy Awards, January 26, 2020.

Fun Facts

In January 2020, Billie became the youngest artist to write and record the theme song for a James Bond movie.

A STYLE ALL HER OWN

Billie became known for wearing oversized, baggy clothing. Her style was the opposite of the typical pop star. She did not want people to say anything about her body.

Billie began her own clothing line. Some of the clothes are made from recycled materials. In 2018, she launched her online clothing store called Blohsh.

As Billie has gotten older, her style has started to change. She wants to wear more fitted clothing. Some of her fans are not happy with her new look. But Billie is deciding what is best for her.

Billie at the Met Gala in 2021

Finneas O'Connell, Billie Eilish, Maggie Baird

Fun Facts

In 2021, Billie released a documentary about herself. She wanted to film it in the same style as her favorite TV show *The Office*. It includes home videos shot by Billie and her family.

GETTING PERSONAL

Billie has opened up about some of her struggles. She lives with Tourette Syndrome, a condition that causes people to have sudden twitches or **tics**. Talking about the disorder has helped Billie better connect with her fans.

Billie also takes a stand on issues she cares about. She encourages her fans to get out and vote. She speaks out about climate change and the environment. She talks about the dangers of **body shaming**.

In just a few years, Billie Eilish has skyrocketed to the top with her music. Her fans are looking forward to seeing what she shares next.

A mural of Billie by artist Emmalene Blake in Dublin, Ireland

GLOSSARY

body shaming (BAA-dee SHAY-mihng): Making critical comments about the shape, size, or appearance of someone's body

documentary (daa-kyoo-MEN-tur-ee): A movie or TV show that tells facts about real people or events

Grammys (GRA-meez): Awards given by the Recording Academy of the United States to recognize achievements in music

lyrics (LEE-ruhks): The words to a song

passionate (PA-shuh-nit): Having or showing strong emotions for something

producer (pruh-DOO-ser): A person who oversees the making of a music recording

single (SING-guhl): A song which is released as a stand-alone item and not as part of an album

soundtrack (SOUND-trak): The music recorded for a movie

tic (TIC): Sudden movements, twitches, or sounds that are done repeatedly

ukulele (yoo-kuh-LAY-lee): A musical instrument with four strings that looks like a small guitar

vegan (VEE-guhn): Using or containing no animal products

viral (VI-rul): Quickly and widely spread online through social media

INDEX

WEBSITES TO VISIT

https://kids.kiddle.co/Billie_Eilish

https://www.biography.com/musician/billie-eilish

https://www.teenvogue.com/video/watch/billie-eilish-creates-the-soundtrack-to-her-life

ABOUT THE AUTHOR

Samantha Bell lives with her family in the foothills of the Blue Ridge Mountains. She has four gray cats with a lot of attitude. When she's not writing, she likes to draw, hike, and visit new places.

Crabtree Publishing

crabtreebooks.com 800-387-7650

Written by: Samantha Bell
Designed by: Kathy Walsh
Series Development: James Earley
Proofreader: Melissa Boyce
Educational Consultant: Marie Lemke M.Ed.
Production manager: Candice Campbell

Hardcover: 978-1-0398-3911-3
Paperback: 978-1-0398-3996-0
Ebook (pdf): 978-1-0398-4068-3
Epub: 978-1-0398-4140-6

Printed in the U.S.A./CP2025

Published in Canada
Crabtree Publishing
616 Welland Ave.
St. Catharines, Ontario
L2M 5V6

Published in the United States
Crabtree Publishing
347 Fifth Ave
Suite 1402-145
New York, NY 10016

Library and Archives Canada Cataloguing in Publication
Available at Library and Archives Canada

Library of Congress Cataloging-in-Publication Data
Available at the Library of Congress

Photographs: Shutterstock, Newscom: Cover, Title pg, backgrounds: DFree@Newscom, Anna Davidovskaya, StockAppeal, Vector Tradition, Miloje; p 5, 7, 16, 17, 19: StockAppeal; p 7, 11, 14, 19, 21, 23: Vector Tradition; p 3: DFree; p 4: DNPhotography/ABACA; p 5: DFree; p 6: Ben Houdijk; p 7: Anthony Behar; p 8: Jeffrey Mayer/Avalonn; p 9: Hutchins Photo; p 10: Justin Higuchi; p 11: GSAA/ZDS; p 12: Dafydd Owen; p 13: Sthanlee B. Mirador; p 14: Zoran Veselinovic; p 15: KH1; p 16: Jen Lowery/Splashnews; p 17: Gonzales Photo/Lasse Lagoni; p 18: Imagespace; p 20: Tsuni/Everett Collection; p 21: Rick Davis/SplashNews; p 22: DFree; p 23: Daniel DeSlover, Moma okgo; p 24: Anthony Behar; p 25: Mark Von Holden/A.M.P.A.S./SplashNews; p 26: manmen studio; p 27: Debby Wong; p 28: @Wiki; p 29: Niall Carson; P 31: Hutchins Photo